A Roadmap
to
Democracy

Maryam Rajavi's Ten-point Plan
for the Future of Iran
in Her Own Words

**A Roadmap to Democracy
Maryam Rajavi's Ten-point Plan for the Future
of Iran in Her Own Words**

*Excerpts of remarks by The President-elect of the NCRI
for the period to transfer sovereignty to the people of Iran*

ISBN: 978-2-491615-11-6

Published May 2023 by
The National Council of Resistance of Iran
15 rue des Gords, 95430 Auvers-sur-Oise, France

Table of Contents

Introduction

A Roadmap to Democracy: Maryam Rajavi's Ten-Point Plan for Iran

The protests that erupted across Iran in September 2022 have profoundly impacted the country's political landscape. This pivotal moment in Iran's history signals that a return to the previous status quo is unlikely. A new balance of power has emerged, with a growing consensus among policymakers that the current regime is facing an existential crisis. Despite its desperate attempts to retain control, the regime appears unable to provide solutions to the problems afflicting the country, putting its very existence at risk.

The crucial question now is what will come after the current regime falls. To answer this question, examining the opposition's proposed program and what steps will be required to ensure its successful implementation after the regime's overthrow is essential.

In 2006, Mrs. Maryam Rajavi, the President-elect of the National Council of Resistance of Iran (NCRI), presented her Ten-Point Plan for Iran's future at the Council of Europe. This comprehensive blueprint envisions a peaceful, prosperous, and democratic nation, resonating with Iranians across various societal backgrounds. As a result, it has gained widespread support from diverse segments of the Iranian population.

The Ten-Point Plan is built upon the principles of democracy, human rights, and the rule of law within a secular and democratic republic. In addition to these core principles, the plan includes several notable features. The plan addresses the most fundamental historical rights, ideals, and pressing needs of the Iranian people in pursuit of a republic grounded in free and fair elections.

The plan is rooted in the comprehensive

program of the National Council of Resistance of Iran, which has been established and announced for four decades. The plan pledges to conduct a free election for the Constituent Assembly within six months following the regime's overthrow. The assembly will be tasked with drafting the constitution for the new republic.

For the first time in Iran's history, no religion will be designated as the official state religion, ensuring that discrimination against adherents of other religions or beliefs is eliminated and maintaining the separation of religion and state.

The Ten-Point Plan is backed by a resistance movement with over four decades of dedication, marked by 120,000 martyrs. The NCRI is the most enduring political coalition in Iran's history, committed to upholding the nation's independence and freedom. The People's Mojahedin Organization of Iran (PMOI/MEK), the council's pivotal constituent, is the sole nationwide movement with a massive organized dedicated network inside the country. It is currently establishing and managing Resistance Units across Iran, with its extensive and growing activities evident to all.

The Ten-Point Plan is not merely a theoretical or academic proposition for an alternative. Both the National Council of Resistance and the People's Mojahedin Organization of Iran have actively demonstrated their commitment to the plan's provisions. For example, both organizations have been fighting for complete gender equality for decades, as advocated by the plan. Similarly, the MEK has played a critical role in exposing the regime's nuclear ambitions over the past two decades, aligning with the plan's vision for a non-nuclear Iran.

This book is a collection of Mrs. Rajavi's speeches, presenting a comprehensive understanding of the plan's principles, vision, and practical implications. It serves as a testament to the importance of presenting a clear and comprehensive program for a serious alternative seeking to establish change, and it highlights the NCRI's commitment to this principle.

Our mission is to cultivate hope and belief and to dismantle the walls of repression. We strive to pave the way for overthrowing religious tyranny and establishing a republic based on freedom, democracy, and equality in Iran. Our ultimate objective is to transfer power to the Iranian people, and we are willing to do whatever it takes to achieve this goal.

Maryam Rajavi

Maryam Rajavi's Ten-point Plan for the Future of Iran

1- Rejection of velayat-e faqih (absolute clerical rule). Affirmation of the people's sovereignty in a republic founded on universal suffrage and pluralism.

2- Freedom of speech, freedom of political parties, freedom of assembly, freedom of the press, and the internet. Dissolution and disbanding of the Islamic Revolutionary Guard Corps (IRGC), the terrorist Qods Force, plainclothes agencies, the unpopular Basij, the Ministry of Intelligence, Council of the Cultural Revolution, and all suppressive patrols and institutions in cities, villages, schools, universities, offices, and factories.

3- Commitment to individual and social freedoms and rights in accordance with the Universal Declaration of Humans Rights. Disbanding all agencies in charge of censorship and inquisition. Seeking justice for murdered political prisoners, prohibition of torture, and the abolishment of the death penalty.

4- Separation of religion and state, and freedom of religions and beliefs.

5- Complete gender equality in the realms of political, social, cultural, and economic rights and equal participation of women in political leadership. Abolishment of any form of discrimination. The right to choose one's own clothing freely, the right to freely marry and divorce, and to obtain education and employment. Prohibition of all forms of exploitation of women under any pretext.

6- An independent judiciary and legal system consistent with international standards based on the presumption of innocence, the right to defense counsel, the right of appeal, and the right to be tried in a public court. Full independence of judges. Abolishment of the mullahs' sharia law and dissolution of Islamic Revolutionary Courts.

7- Autonomy for, and removal of double injustices against Iranian nationalities and ethnicities consistent with the NCRI's Plan for the Autonomy of Iranian Kurdistan.

8- Justice and equal opportunities in the realms of employment and entrepreneurship for all of the people of Iran in a free market economy. Restoration of the rights of blue-color workers, farmers, nurses, white-color workers, teachers and retirees.

9- Protection and rehabilitation of the environment, which has been decimated under the rule of the mullahs.

10-A non-nuclear Iran that is also devoid of weapons of mass destruction. Peace, co-existence and international and regional cooperation.

01

Rejection of velayat-e faqih (absolute clerical rule). Affirmation of the people's sovereignty in a republic founded on universal suffrage and pluralism.

We have rejected the constitution of the velayat-e faqih

The clerical regime has usurped the popular sovereignty of the Iranian people, which is their most critical right. According to the first article of the Platform of the National Council of Resistance of Iran (NCRI), the Provisional Government resulting from the Resistance is "essentially tasked with transferring power to the Iranian people."

This duty shall be fulfilled at the end of a maximum 6-month period after the clerical regime's overthrow by forming a national assembly through free and popular elections, with direct, equal, and secret ballots cast by the Iranian people. As soon as the national assembly has been formed and expresses readiness to fulfill its responsibilities and obligations, the Provisional Government shall hand over its resignation to the assembly.[1]

Popular sovereignty in place of the sovereignty of the Shah or the mullahs

The NCRI is duty-bound to transfer sovereignty

to the people of Iran. The NCRI platform recognizes the people's right to decide their own destiny. It has declared that "achieving popular sovereignty... is the most precious outcome of the Iranian people's just Resistance." It further adds that the prerequisite for popular sovereignty is "to provide and guarantee the equipment, resources, and ways of intervention and participation of all the citizens in making decisions and implementing them."

In fact, the fundamental spirit of the NCRI Platform, the essence of its adopted plans, and the content of its most important statements and declarations are in a word summed up in the principle of popular sovereignty in place of the sovereignty of the Shah or the mullahs.[2]

A constitution that defends freedom, democracy, and equality

With this ideal and this faith, we are determined

We are determined to build a free and democratic society

to build a free and democratic society. A century ago, the Mojahedin of the Constitutional Movement sought to realize "justice, freedom, equality, and unity." Afterward, the great Nationalist leader of Iran, Dr. Mohammad Mossadeq, rose up and proclaimed, "The goal is to facilitate the participation of people in all respects and to empower them to run the country's affairs."

Subsequently, the Fedayeen and the People's Mojahedin Organization of Iran (PMOI/MEK) and other vanguard activists opened the path to overthrow the Shah's dictatorship. And now, our Resistance - with a galaxy of fallen heroes and heroines - from Ashraf Rajavi and Moussa Khiabani to Sedigheh Mojaveri and Neda Hassani, to Zohreh Ghaemi and Giti Givechian - has arisen to ensure freedom of choice for every one of our fellow Iranians.

We have rejected the tyrannical ruling regime. We have rejected a religion based on compulsion and misogyny. And we have rejected the constitution of the velayat-e faqih.

The NCRI is duty-bound to transfer sovereignty to the people of Iran

Our constitution respects freedom, democracy, and equality. It has not been drafted by the Assembly of Experts, a collection of criminals. Today, it is engraved in the hearts of every Iranian. Tomorrow, it will be drafted by elected representatives of the Iranian people in a Constituent Assembly.

That Constitution will be founded on a free, tolerant, and progressive republic. It will rest on pluralism, separation of religion and state, women's equality, and women's active and equal participation in political leadership. It will be founded on the belief in equal rights for all ethnic and religious minorities and a society devoid of torture and executions.[3]

Our roadmap

Our roadmap for realizing the Iranian people's

demands is to struggle to overthrow the clerical regime on all fronts. Our goal is freedom, democracy, equality, and the establishment of a republic based on the separation of church and state.

On this path, we highlight demarcation from the regime in its entirety, and we stress solidarity with all true defenders of its overthrow. The National Council of Resistance of Iran was founded for this purpose: to overthrow the velayat-e faqih regime.

Power and governance belong to the Iranian Republic. Therefore, the only criterion would be a free, direct, equal, and secret ballot cast by the Iranian people.

The clerical regime has usurped the sovereignty of the Iranian people, which is their most critical right.[4]

We are not saying that the mullahs must go so that we can replace them. We are saying that the Iranian people's vote, choice, and opinion must have sovereignty. We are willing to sacrifice ourselves to realize free choice for the Iranian people. This choice will herald trust, freedom, and justice in Iran.

And it shall be so.

You ask what our policy is and what path lies ahead of us. The answer is to carry on the fight in all its forms, everywhere, and with full force.

You ask what our goal is. The answer is to establish freedom, democracy and equality in Iran.

If this struggle faces difficulty and hardship, if it is long and torturous, so be it. We are not afraid, because we have risen to sacrifice all of our being and existence for the cause of the Iranian people's freedom.[5]

A Model for a Democratic Iran

Since the outset, the NCRI President [Massoud Rajavi] has said, "We wish to present a model based on which we can solve all the problems in a post-Khomeini Iran, in a democratic atmosphere, and in line with our people's interests."

The NCRI has pledged not to seek power but to transfer power to the people of Iran. Based on the plans adopted by the National Council of Resistance of Iran, the Provisional Government must hold a free election to form the National Constituent and Legislative Assembly within six months. As far as the Provisional Government is concerned, transferring power to the people will end as soon as the National Constituent and Legislative Assembly is formed.

Among other values, traditions, and democratic methods upheld by the NCRI is the rejection of the balance of power principle in its internal relations. Instead, the NCRI respects the rule of "equal vote" and "one vote for every member," regardless of whether the member represents an organization as big as the PMOI/MEK or is an individual. This method is unprecedented in the history of political coalitions because every coalition is formed based on the balance of power among its member parties. All decisions and agreements are subsequently made based on the same balance of power. As a result, individual personalities and smaller groups do not play a sufficient role.

And all of you have witnessed over the years that the NCRI President has never made any decision without the consensus of all member organizations and personalities. The NCRI relies on debate and

Our goal is freedom, democracy, equality, and the establishment of a republic based on the separation of church and state

persuasion, without any exception, to adopt its plans and documents. This is very significant, particularly since we are in exile and away from our homeland, and preserving the coalition, its unity, and collective progress is extremely difficult.

The Platform of the National Council of Resistance of Iran indicates that everyone must pass the test of "public opinion polls and general elections" and adopt the "free public debates and general consensus" method as much as possible. By offering a progressive platform and groundbreaking plans for the future of a free Iran, the National Council of Resistance of Iran has raised the bar and positively contributed to the progressive nature of the resistance movement and of Iranian society.

The credibility of NCRI plans and documents

emanates from its commitment to a relentless resistance against the clerical regime. They have had a great impact on inspiring progressive generations in Iran and leading them towards freedom.

This constant struggle also provides the dynamism for the NCRI's endurance and growth.

As far as I know, the NCRI is the only example in contemporary political history where the departure, expulsion, or treason of its members or their defection to the regime's camp have been transparently reported to the people of Iran, one by one, via statements, resolutions, publications and particularly, reports by the NCRI President. Never in the past 40 years have we been instigators of a dispute with any individual or any group. As the NCRI President has repeatedly announced on various occasions, we have always been the party to terminate a problem since the sole criterion for us in dealing with any problem is our struggle to overthrow the regime.

This has been particularly so with regard to the individuals who crossed the NCRI's red lines, seeking rapprochement with the mullahs, or those who fell into traps placed by the regime's Intelligence Ministry and later posed as critics of the NCRI and the PMOI/MEK. This has also been one of the high points of the NCRI's history in recent years. There is an old saying that a blacksmith can be trusted only when the sound of his hammer never stops from morning to night. The Iranian people also trust this movement because they constantly and incessantly hear the sound of its hammer during its fight.

To protect the sacrifice and suffering of the people of Iran and their most valiant children and to guarantee Iran's future, the NCRI President offered and founded this alternative, guaranteeing its endurance for 40 years through numerous trials and tribulations and great suffering. The steadfast members and loyal supporters of the NCRI have also shown in the past four decades that they are profoundly aware of this mission. They have shown that to protect this independent alternative, they will not cave into any power or government and will not tolerate the slightest distortion of its principles. They have shown that they will pay any price to protect the boundaries and red lines separating the people of Iran from the religious dictatorship in its entirety.

They have shown that in every storm, every test, every difficulty, and under any pressure, they will not abandon their struggle to overthrow the regime. They give their all for the struggle and resistance for freedom. The NCRI is part of Iran's history. It is, in reality, a political umbrella for the people's struggle to achieve freedom, independence, justice, and economic and social progress.

Iran's future history will pay homage to the special place of the NCRI President and his momentous initiative, as it will be profoundly affected by this democratic alternative and the great contributions it has made to advance the cause of the Iranian people's freedom and sovereignty.

Since its inception, the National Council of Resistance of Iran has proudly remained steadfast in this historic battle. It will remain until the day of victory when sovereignty is transferred to the people of Iran.[6]

Drawing the line with two dictatorships

The Iranian Resistance's experience is a concise summary of the Iranian people's 120-year struggle for freedom. The experience of the Iranian people and Resistance since its outset on June 20, 1981, can be summed up in the phrase "neither the Shah nor the Sheikh (mullahs)." This is the true, essential, and necessary meaning of freedom and independence.[7]

Over the past century, two major currents have evolved in parallel. The first current has been an appallingly despotic regime, founded through the complicity of the monarchic and clerical regimes despite their drastic inherent differences. The second current has been an alternative developing from the heart of the people's front for sovereignty, freedom, and a republic. This is the essence of the history of the past 100 years in Iran.

The NCRI was founded on the basis of "no to the Shah and no to the mullahs"

A review of this history yields another conclusion as well. The model of the monarchy, a model of dependence and despotism, has failed. The religious dictatorship model, a model of religious tyranny, has also failed. The dark despotic rule of Reza Khan abandoned Iran into the clutches of the Allies who occupied the country. His son's dictatorship led to a reactionary religious rule. Khomeini ravaged Iran with an eight-year war and senseless massacres, and genocides. And Khamenei plunged Iran into regional wars, suppression, hunger, and disease.

So both models have failed. And the answer, the solution, is the NCRI, which has emerged on the basis of rejection of foreign dependence and defiance of religious fascism. We all know that the NCRI was founded on the basis of "no to the Shah and no to the mullahs." This demarcation is the rejection of regimes that rely on torture, murder, plunder, treachery, and depravation of the people.

In the face of the dictatorships of the Shah and

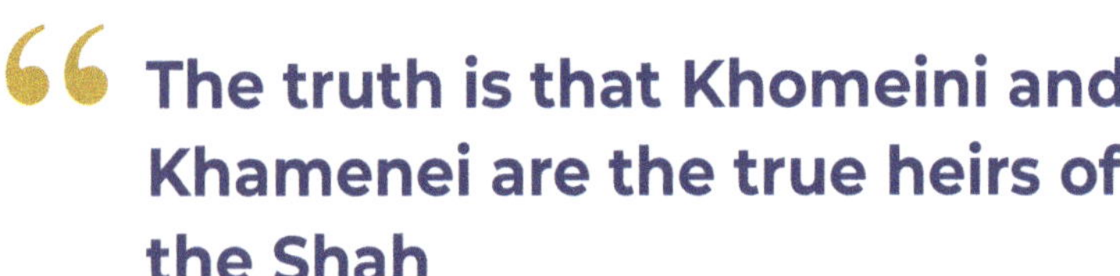

the mullahs, the National Council of Resistance of Iran relies on the principles of freedom and popular sovereignty, which means free choice and an equal vote for all citizens, freedom and democracy, gender equality, the autonomy of ethnic groups, human rights, the people's participation in deciding their own destiny, social and economic justice, and national solidarity. Since the outset, immediately after Khomeini seized power, all these issues have been areas of conflict between us and the ruling reactionary regime.[8]

The Shah and the mullahs: Accomplices in tyranny and oppression

Those who equate the anti-monarchy revolution with the infamous Khomeini rule are distorting history. By reducing Iran's history to a series of dictatorships and authoritarian governments, they ignore the truth of the revolution and overlook the role of the people and their authentic representatives. They fail to recognize the existence of their revolutionary children.

The question remains: Didn't the people of Iran have their own revolutionary force and alternative?

Was their history reduced to a simple choice between king and mullah? What is the truth?

The truth is that Khomeini and Khamenei are the true heirs of the Shah, products of the great error of Western governments that launched the coup against Prime Minister Mossadegh's Nationalist government. That interference closed the path to national and democratic aspirations and paved the way for a reactionary alternative. The current regime is the result of the Shah's treacherous suppression of revolutionary movements, which created a power vacuum that Khomeini filled. Throughout Iran's history, we have witnessed the Shah and the mullahs colluding to establish tyranny and oppression and to exploit the people.

Today, we see that on the one hand, the corrupt manifestations of the former dictatorship, including torturers, have been recruited by the clerical regime. On the other hand, the mercenaries of the mullahs and advocates of the deposed monarchy have come forward to present a false choice to the people of Iran: either monarchy under the Shah or the rule of the clerics, with no place for democracy and popular sovereignty.[9]

The Alternative

When we talk about the alternative, it is not merely a hollow claim or a vague title that has no impact on the daily vicissitudes of the struggle against the regime. Rather, we are referring to the guiding force, the mechanism of advancement that determines the direction of the totality of the actions of the struggle. It clarifies the steps to be taken, the direction, the slogan, the commonalities, and the contradictions, and it sets the priorities.

The alternative represents the solution to every problem the movement faces daily on difficult and rough terrain. It reveals the targets, distinguishes good from bad, differentiates right from wrong, and protects the assets of the Iranian people and Resistance from being stolen by the regime and its accomplices. In a word, the alternative is the yardstick in the struggle for the clerical regime's overthrow.[10]

Phony alternatives

These days, an industry concocting phony

alternatives has become prevalent in the political arena, copying and pasting aspects from elsewhere. And this in itself is another sign of the phase of the regime's overthrow. But the crux is how they will bring down this regime in practice. This question is especially relevant as the blood of the martyrs has permanently and historically blocked the path to reform within the clerical regime and the return of the monarchy.

Now, if one can topple this regime without an organization and leadership, without overcoming thorny trials, and without paying the price and making sacrifices, we say please, go ahead, don't delay.

If one can restore the people's sovereignty without a history of fighting against two regimes, without drawing boundaries against dictatorship,

The alternative represents the solution to every problem the movement faces daily on difficult and rough terrain

subordination and dependency, without waging a nationwide resistance and offering a galaxy of martyrs, without challenging the principle of the velayat-e faqih and phony regime "moderates," we say please, go ahead, don't delay.

If one can topple the mullahs without challenging Khomeini over the unpatriotic Iran-Iraq War, forcing an end to the inferno of that war, and discrediting the regime's slogan of "liberating Qods via Karbala"; without compelling Khomeini to accept the ceasefire by launching 100 military operations by the National Liberation Army of Iran, which captured the city of Mehran and marched to the gates of Kermanshah; and without exposing the regime's nuclear weapons; missile, chemical and microbiological programs and facilities, yes, go ahead and don't delay.

If one can leapfrog a fifty-year history overnight and create real change in Iran while dreaming about foreign support, without having to expose the regime's human rights abuses and crimes in 64 UN resolutions, without the campaign for justice for the massacre of political prisoners in 1988, without campaigns by supporters of the Resistance worldwide insisting on the rights of the Iranian nation for four decades, without the specific platform and programs of the NCRI and the Provisional Government for the transition of sovereignty to the Iranian people, and finally without a tested leader, who has guided this ferocious struggle for five decades, if all this could instead be done overnight, we say go ahead, the ball is in your court.

But let me say this: Such a fantasy is only possible through an Iraq-like occupation, in other words, through foreign intervention. The aftermath of this scenario is already known.

Over the past 40 years, all those aspiring opponents unwilling to pay the price have had opportunities to test their luck. But the hard realities and real experiences have shown that this dark and evil regime will neither be reformed nor turn "green" or "velvet."

The overthrow of this regime inevitably requires a willingness to pay the necessary price. It requires honesty and sacrifice. It requires an organization and a sturdy political alternative. And it requires

We believe that it is with the hands of our people and ours, and with the will of our people and ours, that the dream of freedom will become a political and social reality in Iran

the organization of resistance units and an army of liberation.

Nevertheless, as Massoud Rajavi said in evaluating the January uprising: "We are not in competition with anyone seeking to assume power, on the other hand, and most certainly, no one can compete with the PMOI (MEK) when it comes to practicing honesty, sacrifice and paying the price."

Sixteen years ago, the Iranian Resistance adopted a plan called the National Solidarity Front for the Overthrow of the Ruling Religious Dictatorship and declared that it was prepared to cooperate with all forces who want a republic, who are committed to the complete rejection of the velayat-e faqih regime and who struggle for a democratic, independent Iran, based on separation of religion and state...

It is possible to eradicate high prices, poverty, unemployment, shanty towns, water shortages, and environmental calamities. But, before anything else, the trampled political rights, specifically the right to sovereignty of the Iranian people, must be restored and revived. This is the aim of our Resistance and the raison d'etre for the NCRI.[11]

No hopes pinned on the regime's internal contradictions or its contradictions with the West

We believe that it is with the hands of our people and ours, and with the will of our people and ours, that the dream of freedom will become a political and social reality in Iran. That is why we do not rely on the feuding within religious fascism nor its conflicts with Western governments. As Massoud Rajavi, the Leader of the Iranian Resistance, says, "Since the outset, it was not this or that government in the United States or Europe that was supposed to deliver our freedom on a silver platter. If they are not directly or indirectly aligned with the Shah and the mullahs against us and our nation and do not throw stones at us, that is enough for us."

We bow to any person, party, or group seeking to overthrow the regime and establish freedom in Iran. And we never have and never will give preference to our group's interests over what can more quickly free Iran from its captivity.

It is not our policy to wait and see. On the contrary, we have always taken the initiative. For example, on gender equality, we have already started to implement what we want for tomorrow's society, and we have cherished women's leadership in the ranks of this Resistance. As for a nuclear-free Iran, we have already started working on it and have closed that pathway for the regime. And as for independence, which should be the fundamental principle governing the destiny of our country, we have already started on this path by applying it to ourselves. And we are proud to fly with our wings and rely only on our people.

We have never sacrificed our principles and values for political expediency. If the PMOI had gone along with Khomeini and accepted the constitution of velayat-e faqih, all doors would have been open to them. But everyone saw that when Khomeini asked Massoud Rajavi, a presidential candidate in 1980, to accept the religious fascism's Constitution like other candidates had done to qualify, Massoud immediately announced his withdrawal from the presidential race. In addition to boycotting the referendum on the clerical regime's Constitution, the People's Mojahedin announced they would not vote in the presidential election.

Yes, far be it from the generations of the PMOI to harbor ambitions for power and position, to be Number One!

We have used the term "reactionary" to describe Khomeini and his regime from the beginning and have never backed down. We have never backed down on the notion of freedom. On the contrary, we have insisted on the regime's overthrow for 40 years. And we will press on it mightily and continue to hammer it so hard on the wall of repression that it will crumble, and Iran will be free.

The NCRI's capabilities and competence have been proven in a series of fundamental issues about the fate of the people, the revolution, and

Iran. Iranians have found their worthy answer in this alternative. With this alternative, overthrowing the regime will result in peace, stability, unity, and territorial integrity.

The uprisings of the past few years have proven that Iranians, from Arab compatriots to Kurdish, Baluchi, Turkmen, Qashqai, and Bakhtiari compatriots, are all part of the same body and are united against the enemy of Iran and Iranians, i.e., the religious dictatorship. The National Council of Resistance of Iran has emphasized autonomy within the framework of an indivisible country and its territorial integrity.

Finally, with its set of programs, plans, and views, and especially with its leadership in the battle against religious dictatorship, this alternative provides the answer to the problems of today's struggle and the solution to the issues of tomorrow's Iran.[12]

Notes:

1 - Maryam Rajavi's speech to the Global Convention of Iranians on the anniversary of the anti-monarchical revolution, February 8, 2014; https://www.maryam-rajavi.com/en/maryam-rajavi-worldwide-iranian-communities-convention/

2 - Maryam Rajavi's speech at the 3-day summit of the National Council of Resistance of Iran, marking the 40th anniversary of the NCRI's foundation, July 26, 2020; https://www.maryam-rajavi.com/en/maryam-rajavi-ncri-democratic-alternative-solution-future-iran/

3 - Maryam Rajavi's speech to the Iranian Resistance's Grand Rally in Paris, June 13, 2015; https://www.maryam-rajavi.com/en/maryam-rajavi-democratic-iran-overthrow-religious-dictatorship/

4 - Maryam Rajavi's speech to the Global Convention of Iranians on the anniversary of the anti-monarchical revolution, February 8, 2014; https://www.maryam-rajavi.com/en/maryam-rajavi-worldwide-iranian-communities-convention/

5 - Maryam Rajavi's speech to the Iranian Resistance's Grand Rally, June 22, 2013; https://www.maryam-rajavi.com/en/gathering-in-villepinte-near-paris/

6 - Maryam Rajavi's speech at the 3-day summit of the National Council of Resistance of Iran, July, 2020; https://www.maryam-rajavi.com/en/ncri-founding-anniversary-alternative-mullahs-regime-iran/

7 - Maryam Rajavi's speech to the first session of the Free Iran World Summit, July 10, 2021; https://www.maryam-rajavi.com/en/mullahs-regime-overthrow-democratic-alternative-victory-free-iran-world-summit/

8 - Maryam Rajavi's speech to the three-day NCRI summit, July 26, 2020; https://www.maryam-rajavi.com/en/maryam-rajavi-ncri-democratic-alternative-solution-future-iran/

9 - Maryam Rajavi's speech on the anniversary of the 1979 Revolution, February 6, 2019; https://www.maryam-rajavi.com/en/maryam-rajavi-shah-overthrown-1979-now-turn-mullahs/

10 - Maryam Rajavi's speech on the 41st anniversary of the NCRI's foundation, August 20, 2022; https://www.maryam-rajavi.com/en/ncri-founding-anniversary-alternative-mullahs-regime-iran/

11 - Maryam Rajavi's speech to the first session of the Free Iran World Summit, July 10, 2021; https://www.maryam-rajavi.com/en/regime-overthrow-is-certain-iran-will-be-free/

12 - Maryam Rajavi's speech to the Iranian Resistance's Grand Rally in Paris, June 30, 2018; https://www.maryam-rajavi.com/en/mullahs-regime-overthrow-democratic-alternative-victory-free-iran-world-summit/

02

Freedom of speech, freedom of political parties, freedom of assembly, freedom of the press, and the internet. Dissolution and disbanding of the Islamic Revolutionary Guard Corps (IRGC), the terrorist Qods Force, plainclothes agencies, the unpopular Basij, the Ministry of Intelligence, Council of the Cultural Revolution, and all suppressive patrols and institutions in cities, villages, schools, universities, offices, and factories.

Recognizing individual and social rights

The Iranian people must enjoy all the rights stipulated in the Universal Declaration of Human Rights and other international treaties and conventions, including the International Covenant on Civil and Political Rights, the Convention against Torture, and the Convention to Eliminate All Forms of Discrimination against Women.

Let me also stress the following responsibilities of the Provisional Government, which would take effect on the day that the mullahs are overthrown: Recognition of the individual and social rights of the people as stipulated in the Universal Declaration of Human Rights;

social freedoms, including freedom of assembly, freedom of thought and speech, free press, parties, unions, councils, religions, and faiths; freedom to choose one's occupation; and prevention of all violations against individual and social rights and social freedoms.[1]

While Khomeini refused to make any specific

commitments to establish freedoms, our Resistance and the National Council of Resistance of Iran have consistently rejected vague generalities and clearly announced their commitment to establishing a provisional government on Iranian soil immediately following the downfall of the clerical regime. It aims to present the fruits of the tree of freedom and build a happy, prosperous, and free Iran.

Therefore, in this historic opportunity, while I stand before you -- a segment of the proud and heroic people of Iran -- and in my position of responsibility overseeing the implementation of the National Council of Resistance of Iran's resolutions and the transfer of power to the Iranian people, I would like to cite the ratifications of the National Council of Resistance of Iran and the programs of the provisional government and declare:

1- In tomorrow's Iran, there will be complete freedom of opinion, expression, thought, and the press, and any censorship or inspection of opinions is prohibited.

2- In tomorrow's Iran, political parties, associations, societies, various unions, councils, and organizations, except those loyal to the dictatorships of the Shah and Khomeini, are completely free, and this freedom has no limitations in principle up to armed rebellion against the legitimate and lawful government of the country.

3- In tomorrow's Iran, public elections and votes will form the basis of the legitimacy of the country's ruling system. Laws not adopted by the country's elected legislative authority would not enjoy any credibility or official recognition.

4- In tomorrow's Iran, the judicial and occupational security of all individuals and the individual and social rights stipulated in the Universal Declaration of Human Rights are guaranteed.

5- All repressive institutions surviving from the Khomeini regime will be dissolved in tomorrow's Iran, and all extraordinary courts and tribunals will be disbanded. The principle of the freedom of defense, the right of activity of lawyers' associations, and the handling of crimes in public courts in the presence of a jury are ensured.[2]

[The NCRI advocates] the abrogation and revocation of all suppressive and compulsory measures and forms of discrimination instituted by the clerical regime against Iranian women, including revocation of the denial of the right to freely choose one's occupation and clothing. The recognition of complete gender equality in social, political, cultural, and economic rights.[3]

Iran's people and protestors are determined to establish a republic based on freedom and democracy. They are determined to overthrow the mullahs' religious tyranny. They have decided to do away with the velayat-e faqih constitution and replace it with a constitution based on freedom, equality and democracy. They have decided to topple the Revolutionary Guard Corps and the Basij. They want to invest in the country's education, health, sports, social welfare, jobs and economy instead of investing in nuclear programs and other weapons of mass destruction.

This is our road map. The first step in this road is the overthrow of the clerical regime in its entirety. This is our road map in the name of freedom, for freedom and towards freedom.[4]

Notes:

1- Maryam Rajavi's speech to the Global Convention of Iranians on the anniversary of the anti-monarchical revolution, February 08, 2014; https://www.maryam-rajavi.com/en/maryam-rajavi-worldwide-iranian-communities-convention/

2- Maryam Rajavi's speech at the June 20 Grand Meeting, June 16, 1995

3- Maryam Rajavi's speech to the Global Convention of Iranians on the anniversary of the anti-monarchical revolution, February 08, 2014; https://www.maryam-rajavi.com/en/maryam-rajavi-worldwide-iranian-communities-convention/

4- Maryam Rajavi's speech on the anniversary of the anti-monarchical revolution, February 10, 2018; https://www.maryam-rajavi.com/en/maryam-rajavi-from-1979-revolution-to-the-uprising-in-2018-for-freedom-in-the-name-of-freedom-towards-freedom/

03

Commitment to individual and social freedoms and rights in accordance with the Universal Declaration of Humans Rights. Disbanding all agencies in charge of censorship and inquisition. Seeking justice for murdered political prisoners, prohibition of torture, and abolishing the death penalty.

Human rights in Iran are a victim of diplomacy and trade

We will mark the anniversary of adopting the Universal Declaration of Human Rights in three days. For Iran, Human Rights Day is a reminder of the deep scar on my nation's body and soul, with 120,000 executed dissidents and hundreds of thousands of tortured political prisoners. There are at least 5,000 prisoners on death row and human rights activists and followers of different faiths in prison.

We are determined to remove all forms of suppression and censorship

Under the mullahs, there is no respect for human rights. Unfortunately for the world community and the European Union, human rights in Iran are a victim of diplomacy and trade.

Under the rule of the Iranian regime, every single article of the Universal Declaration of Human Rights has been violated. The right to life, the right to freedom, the right to security, the right to protection from torture and arbitrary arrests, the right to freedom of religion and belief...

The most horrific page in the record of this regime is the massacre of 30,000 political prisoners in only a few months in 1988. This genocide was carried out upon a written edict by Khomeini. The main perpetrators of this massacre are now among the regime's leaders and senior officials.[1]

We are determined to remove all forms of suppression and censorship. This is the pathway that leads to a democratic regime. We are determined to provide the conditions for free choice, for political participation to flourish through freedom of expression and unrestricted activity, and to pave the way for thriving political involvement.

Let us open the gates of the world and all its knowledge and information to Iranian youths.

We insist on the equality of all Iranian citizens; everyone's equality in electing and getting elected; on equality of men and women in all political, social, economic and family rights; and on everyone's enjoyment of equal opportunities for education, higher education, employment and business.

Yes, we are seeking a new order based on freedom, democracy, and equality.[2]

We have risen for an Iran without torture and suppression and devoid of discrimination and inequality. For establishing a democratic republic based on the separation of religion and state, and for a non-nuclear Iran, where the death penalty is abolished. We have risen for an Iran with "an independent judiciary and legal system consistent with international standards based on the presumption of innocence, the right to defense counsel, the right of appeal, full independence of judges, and abolishment of the mullahs' sharia law."

In contrast to the mullahs' cruelty and callousness, we honor compassion and humanity.[3]

An end to the death penalty

The Iranian Resistance has been calling for abolishing the death penalty for years. We emphasize the need for this, and we call on our compatriots to widely protest, more than any

The Iranian Resistance has been calling for abolishing the death penalty for years

other time, the implementation of this inhuman punishment against Iran's youth and those arrested during the uprisings.[4]

Our plan for the future is an Iran without the death penalty and devoid of torture. We plan to put an end to torture and all forms of human rights abuse in Iran. The Iranian Resistance declared years ago that it calls for abolishing the death penalty and ending torture and all forms of rights abuses in Iran. Furthermore, we plan to revive friendship, conciliation, and tolerance.

Our plan for the future is to end the mullahs' religious decrees. We reject the inhuman penal code and other abusive laws of this regime. We believe "retribution" is an inhumane law. Instead, we advocate laws that are based on forgiveness, compassion, and humanity.

The Iranian Resistance's Leader, Massoud Rajavi, ordered the release of thousands of Khomeini's agents arrested in the battles of the National Liberation Army of Iran --many of whom had murdered the PMOI-- without the slightest violation of their human rights.

Yes, this is an enduring tradition of the Iranian people's Resistance. We plan to institute an independent, dynamic, and free judiciary. Our plan is to defend democratic values, freedom, equality, and the sanctity of every citizen's private life.

No one will be arrested arbitrarily. Torture is banned. No defendant shall be deprived of the right to defense and having a defense attorney. The principle of presumption of innocence is respected, and no one, especially no woman, will be deprived of having access to justice when subjected to violence, aggression, and abuse of her freedoms.

Our plan for Iran's future is that no one should be denied their freedoms, rights, or life because of having or not having faith in a particular religion or for abandoning it.

We plan for all citizens to enjoy genuine security and equal rights before the law. We seek a new order based on freedom, democracy, and equality. Therefore, we have chosen to persevere and fight to let our people enjoy a life of freedom and prosperity so that no youngster under 18 years of age would have to wait in the corridors of death in prison to reach the legal age for execution so that no mother will ever shed tears of grief for her executed child.

Our motivation for resistance till victory is not spite and revenge but our love for freedom and human rights. This fuels our steadfastness. And the secret to this endurance is being prepared to sacrifice and pay the price.[5] This plan is not a dream but will undoubtedly become a reality in the future of Iran.

Notes:

1- Maryam Rajavi's speech at the European Parliament, December 7, 2016; https://www.maryam-rajavi.com/en/iran-wave-of-executions-eu-policy-maryam-rajavi-s-speech-at-the-european-parliament-brussels-7-december-2016/

2- Maryam Rajavi's message on the beginning of the new academic year, 2015-2016

3- Maryam Rajavi's message on the International Day Against the Death Penalty, October 9, 2021; https://www.maryam-rajavi.com/en/world-day-against-the-death-penalty/

4- Maryam Rajavi's speech at the 3-day summit of the National Council of Resistance of Iran marking the 40th anniversary of the NCRI's foundation, July 23-26, 2020; https://www.maryam-rajavi.com/en/maryam-rajavi-ncri-democratic-alternative-solution-future-iran/

5- Maryam Rajavi's speech on the World Day against the Death Penalty, October 10, 2015; https://www.maryam-rajavi.com/en/maryam-rajavi-plan-iran-without-death-penalty/

04

**Separation of religion
and state,
and freedom of religions
and beliefs.**

A democratic republic based on the separation of religion and state

Our nation needs to end tyranny under the cloak of religion and establish a democratic republic based on the separation of religion and state, where its oppressed nationalities can achieve their violated rights, including autonomy within Iran's unity and territorial integrity.[1]

The NCRI's response to the experience of religious fascism and barbaric despotism under the banner of Islam is twofold. First, the NCRI Platform, drafted in 1981, underscores "equal political and social rights of all citizens" and seeks to abolish "all gender, ethnic and religious privileges." Of course, the mere formation of the NCRI and the relations among its forces serve as a practical model of separation of religion and state and a republic based on freedom and equality.

The Plan on the Provisional Government's Relations with Religion, adopted by the NCRI in November 1985, denounces all religious coercion and compulsion to practice religion. It further rejects all forms of "discrimination as well as any political or social privileges or coercion" in relation to Islam. On the one hand, the Plan stipulates that "under no circumstance is any religion or denomination recognized as possessing special privileges or rights"; on the other, it underlines "the freedom of religions and beliefs."

The Plan emphasizes in its first article that "All forms of discrimination against the followers of various religions and beliefs in the enjoyment of their individual and social rights are prohibited. No citizens shall enjoy any privileges or be subject to any deprivations in respect of nomination for election, voting, employment, education, becoming a judge, or any other individual or social rights, for the reason of belief or non-belief in a particular religion or faith."

> **The PMOI's crucial breakthrough has been its promotion of the separation of religion and state, which leaves no room for theocracy**

In Article 3, the Plan stipulates that "Jurisdiction of judicial authorities is not based upon their religious or ideological stance, and laws not formulated within the legislative institution of the land will have no official sanction or validity."

With these declarations, the NCRI has managed to resolve an issue which dates back to the first Iranian parliament after the Constitutional Revolution in 1906. At that time, during debates over amendments to the Constitution, a major division took place in the parliament between supporters of the Constitution and defenders of the rule of law and democracy on the one hand, and supporters of theocracy and predecessors of the current ruling mullahs, such as Sheikh Fazlollah Nouri, on the other.

Support for a theocratic regime finally led to the despotic rule of velayat-e faqih under the banner of religion, something that the people of Iran have been experiencing for 42 years with their flesh and blood.

In diametric opposition to this theocratic regime, the People's Mojahedin Organization of Iran (PMOI/MEK), which is a member of the NCRI, represents a tolerant Islam -- the antithesis of Khomeini's reactionary outlook, and the ignorant, reactionary ideology represented by him and the velayat-e faqih regime. When the PMOI/MEK movement, with such a progressive outlook, endorses the abolishment of all religious-based privileges, it lends strong, serious backing to the NCRI Plan on the separation of religion and state, and starkly distinguishes it from the customary groundless rhetoric.[2]

A critical milestone

The PMOI's crucial breakthrough has been its promotion of the separation of religion and state, which leaves no room for theocracy and religious discrimination. Support for this principle could not have attained the significance and impact that it has had if it were not initiated by a Muslim movement. Throughout the Middle East and Muslim countries, this serves as the only example where a Muslim resistance movement has been able to defend the principle of separation of religion and state and open the way for the establishment of democracy.

In defense of this principle, we have risen up against coercive religion and religious coercion. Can this principle be considered as creating limitations or introducing revisions to Islam's fundamental ideas? No, to the contrary, it insists on the true spirit of Islam, which in the words of Massoud Rajavi, "takes exception to any justification or legitimacy, including political legitimacy, born out of coercion and compulsion... We profoundly believe that Islam's true blossoming becomes possible when no social or political discrimination, privilege, or coercion is involved."

By the separation of religion and state, do we mean that in a society liberated from dictatorship no individual or group identifying as Islamic can be active? No, what we mean is that, just as the resolution adopted by the National Council of Resistance of Iran says, the ballot box reigns supreme and no privilege should be granted or taken away due to belief or lack of belief in a particular religion. This principle also guarantees freedom of religion in the sense that Muslims or followers of other faiths can freely practice their religion without facing any form of inequality whatsoever.

In a document he prepared in 633 in the city of Medina, the Prophet of Islam said, "Jews and Muslims are like one nation or people. (The only difference is that) the Jews follow their religion and the Muslims are committed to their own."

What we are advocating is to annul and reject tyranny under the veil of religion. This is the conclusion reached from a great historical experience, which foresaw the defeat of religious dictatorship in Iran. Our goal is to overthrow the foundation of sectarianism under the guise of Shiism or Sunnism. Exploiting religion for the pursuit of power must not continue any longer.[3]

The NCRI's Plan

At the height of Khomeini's religious hysteria in the 1980s, the PMOI emphasized the separation of religion and state in the framework of the Plan by the National Council of Resistance of Iran (NCRI). At that time, Massoud [Rajavi] said that adopting this plan was "a source of special pride for all followers of Prophet Mohammad and Imam Ali." Two years earlier, he had said, "Unlike Khomeini, we have not tried to impose our ideology and beliefs on any person or group; we do not and will not do so. We recognize the free vote of the Iranian people as the only criterion of legitimacy and political power."[4]

Our beliefs

As a Muslim woman, while stressing the need for separation of religion and state, and on behalf of a generation that has been defending the genuine Muhammadan Islam against fundamentalism and religious dictatorship for the past five decades, I declare:

1. We reject compulsory religion and any compulsion in religion. Despotism under the name of Islam, the medieval Sharia laws, and the ex-communication of opponents, whether Shiite or Sunni, are against Islam and the liberating Muhammadan religion.

2. In our view, the essence of Islam is freedom, freedom from all forms of compulsion, oppression, and exploitation.

3. We follow genuine Islam, a tolerant and democratic Islam that defends popular sovereignty and gender equality.

4. We reject religious discrimination and will support the rights of followers of all religions and denominations.

5. Our Islam believes in brotherhood among

One of Iran's most significant historical contradictions resolved in recent decades has been the separation of religion and state, championed by a movement that believes in democratic Islam

all religions. Sectarian wars and sowing discord among Shiites and Sunnis are the sinister products of the fundamentalist regime in Iran, which seeks to prolong its anti-Islamic and anti-human caliphate.

Indeed, our God is the God of freedom, our Muhammed is the Prophet of compassion and emancipation, and our Islam is the religion that respects freedom of choice.[5]

A historical contradiction

One of Iran's most significant historical contradictions resolved in recent decades has been the separation of religion and state, championed by a movement that believes in democratic Islam.

Emphasizing this principle is not a new idea for the Iranian Resistance. It has been guaranteed in the National Council of Resistance's program, published by Massoud Rajavi in November 1981.

In November 1985, the NCRI demonstrated its leadership and direction in this area by adopting and publishing a Plan emphasizing two fundamental pillars: the right to religious freedom and the rejection of any special rights or privileges for any religion or denomination.

Then it presents a framework consisting of four articles: First, prohibit discrimination against followers of different religions and denominations. Second, banning any compulsory religious or ideological education. Third, not recognizing any law that does not originate from the country's legislative authority and emphasizing that the religious and ideological affiliation of judicial officials does not confer special authority—fourth, prohibiting government authorities' inspection of personal beliefs and religions.

In the message he simultaneously published, Massoud Rajavi described the approval of this plan as a source of "special pride for all followers of the true Islam of Mohammad and Ali."

This is the essence of democratic Islam in the face of religious coercion and clerical rule.[6]

A demand of the Iranian people

The NCRI's platform for establishing a republic based on freedom and democracy, universal suffrage, the separation of religion and state, gender equality, and the autonomy of ethnic groups has received more popular approval than ever before. The NCRI has also achieved many successes in the daily struggle to expose the regime's vulnerability and deadlocks on the verge of overthrow. It has shown that the NCRI is the alternative and the solution and promises a viable, concrete prospect.

The Resistance units have consistently targeted the mullahs' religious seminaries and centers, thereby highlighting two facts: One is the Iranian people's disgust with the mullahs' religious propaganda, and the other is the people's desire to separate religion from the state, a desire that the NCRI has reflected for 40 years.[7]

Notes:

1- Maryam Rajavi's speech at the European Parliament, December 7, 2016; https://www.maryam-rajavi.com/en/iran-wave-of-executions-eu-policy-maryam-rajavi-s-speech-at-the-european-parliament-brussels-7-december-2016/

2- Maryam Rajavi's message on the beginning of the new academic year, 2015-2016

3- Maryam Rajavi's message on the International Day Against the Death Penalty, October 9, 2021; https://www.maryam-rajavi.com/en/world-day-against-the-death-penalty/

4- Maryam Rajavi's speech at the 3-day summit of the National Council of Resistance of Iran marking the 40th anniversary of the NCRI's foundation, July 23-26, 2020; https://www.maryam-rajavi.com/en/maryam-rajavi-ncri-democratic-alternative-solution-future-iran/

5- Maryam Rajavi's speech on the World Day against the Death Penalty, October 10, 2015; https://www.maryam-rajavi.com/en/maryam-rajavi-plan-iran-without-death-penalty/

6 - Maryam Rajavi's speech at an Iftar ceremony at Ashraf-3, March 25, 2023; https://www.maryam-rajavi.com/en/ramadan-peace-friendship-middle-east-world-islam/

7 - Maryam Rajavi's speech at the NCRI session, July 2022; https://www.maryam-rajavi.com/en/ncri-founding-anniversary-alternative-mullahs-regime-iran/

05

Complete gender equality in the realms of political, social, cultural, and economic rights and equal participation of women in political leadership. Abolishment of any form of discrimination. The right to choose one's clothing freely, the right to voluntarily marry and divorce, and to obtain education and employment. Prohibition of all forms of exploitation against women under any pretext.

The Plan on Women's Rights and Freedoms

In 1987, the National Council of Resistance (NCRI) unanimously adopted a plan for the rights and freedoms of women in Iran. In March 2010, Maryam Rajavi presented the Iranian Resistance's perspective during a meeting at the European Parliament entitled "Women Pioneer Democratic Change in Iran."

A - Principles:

First: Abolishing and eliminating all forms of oppression, coercion, and discrimination imposed on Iranian women by the mullahs' reactionary regime and their sharia law. Adhering to all freedoms and rights of women as stipulated in the Universal Declaration of Human Rights, the Convention on the Elimination of All Forms of Discrimination against Women, and the Declaration on the Elimination of Violence Against Women, which the United Nations General Assembly approved in December 1993

Second: Emphasizing complete equality of

social, political, cultural, and economic rights between men and women.

Third: Ensuring the complete provision of women's rights in the country, without regard to any unequal and discriminatory practices or limitations and rejecting any perception that views women as commodities.

Women's rights are defined

1. The right to elect and be elected in all elections and suffrage in all referendums.

2. The right to employment, free choice of profession, and the right to hold any public or government position or office, including the presidency and political leadership, and judgeship in all judicial institutions.

3. The right to free political and social activity, social intercourse, and travel without another person's permission.

4. The right to freely choose clothing and attire.

5. The right to use, without discrimination, all instructional, educational, athletic, and artistic resources; and the right to participate in all athletic competitions and artistic activities.

6. Recognition of women's associations and support for their voluntary formation throughout the country. Consideration of special privileges in various social, administrative, cultural, and particularly educational fields to abolish inequality and the dual oppression of women.

7. Equal pay for equal work; prohibition of discrimination in hiring and during employment; equal access to various privileges such as vacation, retirement benefits, and disability compensation; enjoyment of child and spousal benefits and unemployment insurance; the right to salary and special accommodations during pregnancy, childbirth, and infant care.

8. Absolute freedom of choice of spouse and marriage, which can take place only with the consent of both sides and must be registered with legal authority. Marriage before the attainment of the legal age is prohibited. In family life, any form of compulsion or coercion of the wife is forbidden.

9. Same right to divorce as men. Qualified judicial authorities should handle divorce proceedings. Child custody and support, as well as financial settlements, will be determined by the verdict of the divorce proceedings.

10. Support for widowed and divorced women

and children in their custody. Care will be provided through the National Social Welfare System.

11. Eliminating legal inequalities regarding testimony, guardianship, custody, and inheritance. Polygamy is prohibited.

12. Prohibition of all forms of sexual exploitation of women under any pretext and abrogation of all customs, laws, and provisions allowing the father, mother, guardian, or another to give away a girl or a woman for marriage or other reasons.

These principles, rights, and freedoms are not focused solely on women's emancipation but also on the historical emancipation of Iranian men and women.[1]

Women a force for change and progress

Women's leading role in the fight against fundamentalism doubly serves the movement for equality and the effort to uproot sexual discrimination. The only way to propel that movement forward is to link it with a progressive political   movement.

If women have no share in political power; if they are not part of the leadership and the decision-making processes on social issues; if they do not have a serious, equal role in economic management; and if they are not actively and visibly involved in international politics, all the talk about equality between women and men rings hollow. Absolute equality only comes when women take on critical roles in tackling the primary challenges of the day.

To overturn the system of gender discrimination and bring about fundamental change, women must predominate political leadership for a specific period. Such a predominant role in leadership aims to guarantee equality and uproot sexual oppression, not to replace patriarchy with matriarchy. Thus, all the prerequisites and consequences are liberating in their essence. Once the oppression has been eradicated, the energies thus set free will break through the impasse currently confronting human society and will help to establish a new system of human relations, both within a community and on a global scale.[2]

Against the compulsory veil

Another area of violence and compulsion in Iran is the mandatory dress code or hijab. Since the early days of Khomeini's rule, Iranian women have protested against compulsory veiling. At the time, the PMOI women actively participated in demonstrations against compulsory veiling.

A series of laws were devised to deprive Iranian women of their individual and social rights. Several agencies are in charge of suppression and are specially tasked to counter improper veiling. They have turned Iran into a vast prison for women.

For this reason, we reiterate that Iranian women must be free! They must be free to choose what they believe in, what they want to wear, and how they want to live. And we repeat: NO to compulsory veil, NO to compulsory religion, and NO to compulsory government.[3]

Compulsory hijab, a tool to impose the monopolistic rule of the velayat-e faqih

Misogyny is at the core of society's suppression since preserving the ruling theocracy is predicated on it. Such misogyny does not arise from blind religious zealotry, efforts to safeguard societal chastity, or even efforts to protect the family's foundation. On the contrary, Misogyny under the cloak of religion has become systematic and persistent because it is a lever to maintain the monopolistic domination of the velayat-e faqih.

Misogyny is the raison d'être for dozens of the regime's suppressive agencies. It justifies the permanent surveillance operations in the streets, the actions of street patrols, and the conduct of such agencies as the "Office to Combat Vice," or the "Morality Police," and 20 other police entities.

Similarly, clamping down on women on the pretext of mal-veiling is one of the most effective means to repress society and silence any voice of dissent. The mullahs have no scruples about enchaining women on so-called religious grounds. In other words, they have free rein in scrutinizing and controlling everything, everywhere, including in sports, administrative and production settings, in hiring or firing, in constantly controlling women's and youths' commutes in the streets, in arbitrary raids on people's homes; in censoring books, movies, theater, and music; in filtering websites and social media, in fabricating judicial cases and in attacking social gatherings.

This explains why enforcing the hijab has gained prominence in the regime's policies and laws. This explains why the mullahs openly equate a "mal-veiled" woman with being counterrevolutionary. This explains why whenever the regime suffers a political setback on the international scene or faces social protests and uprisings, it intensifies executions and the campaign against mal-veiling.

The ruling mullahs know that if they show leniency vis-à-vis compulsory veiling or modify any of their laws and policies that oppress women, the latter's power will quickly advance and mobilize society. Indeed, ensuring that the velayat-e faqih regime is secure is the second important reality that helps us understand why the mullahs' misogynous mindset exists.[4]

 **we reiterate that Iranian women must be free! They must be free to choose what they believe in, what they want to wear, and how they want to live**

Compulsory hijab the flipside of forced Removal of the hijab

Reza Shah forced the removal of women's head coverings, while Khomeini imposed it. Thus, the main issue is coercion and dictatorship, leaving no room for free choice. But today, a democratic revolution is unfolding in Iran. Defiant girls from Tehran to Zahedan shout, "With or without the hijab, onward to the revolution!" They want a democratic republic without a turban or crown, defined by freedom, popular sovereignty, and free elections. They demand that retrogression and dictatorship be eradicated, while the mullahs seek to prevent women from playing a crucial role in overthrowing the religious dictatorship in Iran.[5]

Women's active, equal participation in political leadership

It is correct to say that women's rights are human rights, and I firmly believe that women's leadership guarantees democracy and equality. Without opportunities for women to participate in political leadership, any progress toward gender equality is vulnerable to regression.

Today, in their leadership positions and alongside Iranian men, Iranian women are at the forefront of the movement to defeat religious dictatorship and secure freedom, democracy, and equality for tomorrow. The uprising in Iran, led by women, has proved this truth. The rebellion, blazing more fiercely than ever, will make it shine brighter than ever and bring the message of victory and triumph.[6]

Our experience has made it clear that defeating

NO to compulsory veil, NO to compulsory religion, and NO to compulsory government

the curse of inequality is impossible without first leaping: leadership responsibilities must be given to the most competent women without the slightest anxiety. Women's hegemony in the Iranian Resistance, as a paradigm-shifting transformation, paved the way for women to take on responsibilities in all fields.

This, of course, was not meant to strip men of responsibility and to marginalize them. Instead, the objective was to compensate for centuries of male-dominated modus operandi, which barred women from extracting and exercising their abilities to lead.

As a result of this campaign, women succeeded in adopting noble values and rose above a decadent and reactionary culture. As a first accomplishment, they came to believe in themselves and their capabilities. And when they discovered how vital their responsible roles are in advancing the struggle against religious tyranny, they decided to leave the world of irresponsibility and passivity, where a woman's self-identity relies on others. Instead, they stepped into a world of responsible women who, in fact, lead a struggle with all its potential consequences.

They parted with vices that would hold them back, like jealousy, rivalry, and attributing worth to physical attributes, appearance, and age, which significantly deplete women's energies. They also managed to replace attitudes of frailty and fragility with a sense of forte and strength. They shed their fears of facing defeat or exhibiting weakness in difficulties. Instead of succumbing to pressure, they learned to cultivate their power to overcome failure. Instead of losing hope, they learned to remain helpful and persistent in opening the path to victory.

In our movement, relations among women have changed so that women stand alongside each other and support and hear one another as if they were biological sisters. They fulfill the most cumbersome responsibilities collectively and based on such relations. They do not undermine each other. On the contrary, progress made by any of them is a source of encouragement and inspiration for other women. The collective effort to elevate the responsibilities of other women is considered a virtue.

Each woman in the Resistance has realized that

by cooperating with and supporting her colleagues, she will actually be empowering herself. In doing so, they have attained an incredible ability to make sacrifices for their sisters.

Although our point of departure in this transformation was to overthrow the religious fascism ruling Iran to rebuild the free Iran of tomorrow, we must still be armed with this outlook to create democratic institutions in our society. In other words, the Iranian Resistance also has the historic responsibility to be a builder and a founder. Suppose democracy is not built on gender equality, participation of all people, free choice of all sectors of society, and unconditional freedom of speech. In that case, it will quickly deviate and take on reactionary tendencies.

The idea of equality in our movement is inspirational and holds a promise for Iranian society, especially its women and youth. When you target sexism, you are attempting to shatter the cornerstone of the velayat-e faqih system. When you target the mullahs' misogyny, you are aiming at the heart of their ideology. As a result, neither the mullahs' jurisprudence, their sharia, nor their reactionary laws and culture will find a solid footing.

This explains why the mullahs target the PMOI incessantly and extensively through utter demagoguery. In their view, the PMOI's first offense is its unwavering commitment to regime change in Iran. But in addition to this, by the mullahs' sharia, the Iranian Resistance has committed the cardinal sin of believing that Iranian women are competent enough to, and indeed must, assume the leadership of the democratic Iran of tomorrow.

According to the regime's sharia, the PMOI (MEK) has committed a cardinal sin because, in contrast to the mullahs' reactionary ideology, they believe that men are not intrinsically deprived of willpower and are not slaves of their primal instincts. And they also believe that the desire to establish supremacy and commit violence against women considered virtues in the mullahs' religious jurisprudence and sharia, have no place whatsoever in Islam.

Because of such unforgivable "sins," with endless rage and vengeance, the mullahs slander the PMOI and call it a "cult" while continuing to suppress them. They have made the PMOI the target of a campaign of demonization and misinformation for many years because this movement rejects the ruling ideology and behavior and has risen to overthrow oppression, inequality, and injustice.[7]

Women in the PMOI's Central Council

I have always maintained that our resistance movement, especially the 1,000 PMOI women who comprise the PMOI's Central Council, has been forged through years of struggle, sacrifice, and determination. We are driven not by a desire for power but rather to empower the Iranian people, to wrest power from the oppressors who have held it in an authoritarian grip, and to return it to its rightful owners - the people.

This goal is worth any sacrifice, no matter how great, and demands relinquishing personal comfort and security. The 1,000 women who constitute the core of the collective leadership of the Iranian people's uprising and the strategy of 1,000 Ashrafs have embraced a selfless ethos, rejecting the mantras of "me first" and "all for me."

The practical experience and struggle against the Shah and the mullahs made this selfless ethos possible, particularly when thousands of

PMOI women and girls stood on the frontlines to resist Khomeini and his regime. I remember their courageous parade in Tehran and tireless campaigning for Massoud Rajavi's presidential platform that championed freedom. They were imprisoned, tortured, and executed in the thousands, but they refused to be broken and became a shining example of resistance in Iran's modern history.

In difficult moments, when they had to shoulder the burden of heavy responsibilities in positions of authority, I witnessed how they made vital choices by overcoming doubt and disbelief and performed their duties.

During the struggle against regression and dictatorship, I witnessed how the ideologies of sexism and self-centeredness were vanquished. The traditional world of jealousy and rivalry was shattered, giving way to a new era of true sisterhood, mutual support, and cooperation. This is one of the most beautiful moments for me and all women. I dare say that they have come together as a collective, driven by passion and determination for the real progress brought about by overthrowing the oppressive mullahs' regime and establishing a free, democratic, prosperous, and developed Iran where women have equal participation.

Anyone slightly familiar with this experience knows that walking this path is complex and involves confronting severe contradictions at every step. However, these women do not compete with one another; instead, they complement and support each other. They recognize that their strength lies in amplifying their power together rather than eliminating each other. This is the humane and liberating chemistry that every individual needs.

The most significant accomplishment of the Mojahedin women, which has attracted a new generation of revolutionary women over the past four decades, is their ability to create relationships based on empathy instead of narrow-mindedness and jealousy. Their selfless sacrifice for each other knows no limits.

In short, this is what Iranian society's betrayed trust and wounded emotions need. I have witnessed how the path paved by these women has transformed the men within this movement, teaching them to move away from the world of «me first» and rivalry and embrace the world of brotherhood, solidarity, and support. This has resulted in a new generation of thousands of liberated men.[8]

Notes:

1- Maryam Rajavi's speech at the European Parliament, December 7, 2016; https://www.maryam-rajavi.com/en/iran-wave-of-executions-eu-policy-maryam-rajavi-s-speech-at-the-european-parliament-brussels-7-december-2016/

2- Maryam Rajavi's message on the beginning of the new academic year, 2015-2016

3- Maryam Rajavi's message on the International Day Against the Death Penalty, October 9, 2021; https://www.maryam-rajavi.com/en/world-day-against-the-death-penalty/

4- Maryam Rajavi's speech at the 3-day summit of the National Council of Resistance of Iran marking the 40th anniversary of the NCRI's foundation, July 23-26, 2020; https://www.maryam-rajavi.com/en/maryam-rajavi-ncri-democratic-alternative-solution-future-iran/

5- Maryam Rajavi's speech on the World Day against the Death Penalty, October 10, 2015; https://

www.maryam-rajavi.com/en/maryam-rajavi-plan-iran-without-death-penalty/

6 - Maryam Rajavi's speech to the International Women's Day gathering, March 4, 2023; https://www.maryam-rajavi.com/en/conference-international-women-day-democracy-equality/

7 - Maryam Rajavi's speech to the conference on International Women's Day, March 9, 2013; https://www.maryam-rajavi.com/en/speech-at-international-womens-day-conference-2013/

8 - Maryam Rajavi's speech to the International Women's Day gathering, March 4, 2023; https://www.maryam-rajavi.com/en/conference-international-women-day-democracy-equality/

06

An independent judiciary and legal system consistent with international standards based on the presumption of innocence, the right to defense counsel, the right of appeal, and the right to be tried in a public court. Complete independence of judges. Abolishment of the mullahs' sharia law and dissolution of the Islamic Revolutionary courts.

Judicial and occupational security in tomorrow's Iran

In tomorrow's Iran, judicial and occupational security will be guaranteed for all people, and individual and social rights specified in the Universal Declaration of Human Rights will be ensured. All repressive institutions left over from the Khomeini regime and all special courts and tribunals will be dissolved in tomorrow's Iran. The freedom of defense and the right to operate bar associations will be safeguarded, and charges will be examined in open courts in the presence of juries.

The people of Iran are denied "the right to an effective remedy by the competent national tribunals" (article 8 of the Universal Declaration of Human Rights). No such courts exist in Iran. The courts do not observe due process and act at the whim of religious judges, torturers, and suppressive agents.

Article 167 of the regime's Constitution subjected the fate and the rights of the accused and the plaintiffs to the personal whims and intentions of judges

In tomorrow's Iran, judicial and occupational security will be guaranteed for all people, and individual and social rights specified in the Universal Declaration of Human Rights will be ensured

appointed by the mullahs' Supreme Leader. Judges can decide based on their interpretation of the so-called "credible fatwas" -- the alias for Khomeini's book, Tahrir Al-Vasileh.

Those arrested do not enjoy any rights. Trials do not last more than a few minutes, even in sensitive cases where death sentences are issued. Many defendants do not have lawyers or have to accept court-appointed lawyers who often act against the interests of their clients. In some cases, lawyers are denied access to the files of their clients, and if they insist, they will be prosecuted and sometimes sentenced to long prison terms.[1]

Notes:

1- Maryam Rajavi's statement on the 70th anniversary of the Universal Declaration of Human Rights, December 2017; https://www.maryam-rajavi.com/en/declaration-by-maryam-rajavi-on-the-70th-anniversary-of-the-adoption-of-the-universal-declaration-of-human-rights/

07

Autonomy for and removal of double injustices against Iranian nationalities and ethnicities consistent with the NCRI's Plan for the Autonomy of Iranian Kurdistan.

Autonomy of the oppressed ethnic minorities

Another issue the NCRI has tackled since its inception is the autonomy of the oppressed ethnic minorities. Of course, since the beginning of Khomeini's rule, the groups and forces which later made up the National Council of Resistance of Iran stood up against the regime's suppression of our Kurd, Arab, Turkman, and other ethnic compatriots.

The NCRI underlines in its Plan that all ethnic groups and nationalities of our country will enjoy internal autonomy. The Plan also underscores that their cultural, social, and political rights and freedoms are provided within the country's unity, national sovereignty, and territorial integrity.

All ethnic groups and nationalities of our country will enjoy internal autonomy

Specifically, the NCRI drew up a 12-point Plan for the Autonomy of Iranian Kurdistan, adopted in 1983. After three decades, it remains one of the world's most comprehensive models in this regard.[1]

All rights and freedoms stipulated in the Universal Declaration of Human Rights and international covenants relating to them, such as freedom of thought and expression, freedom of the press, freedom of assembly and activity of political parties and organizations, workers,' peasants,' and other professional unions and councils and democratic associations; freedom to choose one's profession and place of residence and freedom of religion are guaranteed in autonomous Kurdistan, just as in other parts of Iran. All residents of Kurdistan, like residents of other parts of Iran, will enjoy social, economic, political, and cultural equality without any discrimination based on gender, ethnicity, race, or religion.[2]

We hold that the existence of ethnic minorities in Iran comprises a tremendous and effective force for toppling the mullahs' regime and achieving freedom. Therefore, we should value the multi-cultural and multi-lingual character of our nation. Our compatriots from different nationalities, cultures, and languages must be able to participate equally in national decision-making. They must preserve their cultural, religious, and lingual identity. They must be able to speak, work and study in their mother tongues and promote them.[3]

The NCRI has strongly reinforced the bonds between the oppressed ethnic minorities and the nationwide opposition through its actions and reactions. In addition, it has drawn public attention to the fact that this democratic alternative is the only source of support for our Baluch, Kurd, and Arab compatriots   nationwide.

Countering the regime's decision to divide Sistan-and-Baluchestan into four provinces, the Resistance denounced the plan as a move to "sow discord in Sistan-and-Baluchestan," and called on the valiant Baluchis to rise against it.

The NCRI strongly opposed the plan to divide the province of Khuzestan in two and encouraged our compatriots in Khuzestan to protest against this plan, which only distracts attention from the uprising and sowed divisions among the people of the province.

In the wake of the regime's bombing of some regions in Iraqi Kurdistan, the NCRI chairman said, "To push back against the mullahs' regime in the bombing of innocent people and Iranian Kurdish parties in the border region, people must rise in the oppressed cities of Iranian Kurdistan and throughout the country, as they did in the case of water shortages in Khuzestan."

During the uprising in Khuzestan, the NCRI Chairman emphasized the destructive role of the IRGC and said, "Khamenei's IRGC must stop deliberately drying up the marshes, which causes environmental disasters, especially for our Arab compatriots."[4]

The clerical regime is the adversary of all the people of Iran, regardless of their ethnicity or background, be it Persian, Turk, Kurd, Arab, Baluch, or others. In terms of suppression, all citizens of Iran find themselves in the same precarious situation. Therefore, while some of our fellow compatriots suffer from the national and religious oppression and discrimination enforced by the regime, it is imperative to bring about this regime's downfall to end all such injustices.

From the outset, the National Council of Resistance

has emphasized the need to eradicate the double oppression against all the diverse ethnic groups of Iran while ensuring their full cultural, social, and political rights and freedoms within the framework of the country's unity, sovereignty, and indivisibility. We emphasize national autonomy. Internal autonomy entails eradicating this double oppression...[5]

Notes:

1- Maryam Rajavi's speech to the 3-day session of the National Council of Resistance of Iran on the 40th anniversary of the NCRI's foundation – July 23-26, 2020; https://www.maryam-rajavi.com/en/maryam-rajavi-ncri-democratic-alternative-solution-future-iran/

2- Plan of the National Council of Resistance of Iran for the Autonomy of Iranian Kurdistan

3- Maryam Rajavi's message on the new academic year 2015-2016

4- Maryam Rajavi's speech to the NCRI session on the 41st anniversary of its founding, July 2022; https://www.maryam-rajavi.com/en/ncri-founding-anniversary-alternative-mullahs-regime-iran/

5- Maryam Rajavi's interview with Al-Majalleh, March 2011

08

Justice and equal opportunities in the realms of employment
and entrepreneurship for all of the people of Iran in a free market economy. Restoration of the rights of blue-color workers, farmers, nurses, white-color workers, teachers, and retirees.

Abolition of anti-labor and anti-peasant laws

Under the mullahs' rule, the people of Iran are deprived of the right to form independent blue and white-collar workers' syndicates, trade unions, and independent student associations. Instead, the clerical regime has created phony unions, part of its security and intelligence apparatus, to control blue and white-collar workers and students.

Many who tried to form independent associations, particularly workers and teachers, have been arrested, sentenced to long-term imprisonment, and deprived of their social rights.

The people of Iran suffer from significant discrimination under the clerical regime. Members of the ruling factions have taken over everything and accumulated astronomical wealth and status. They are exempted from paying taxes and enjoy countless benefits in every field.

No administrative or security red tape affects

them, and they are never prosecuted for their numerous violations and corruption. In contrast, the more significant majority of the people of Iran are always the inferior party in the so-called courts and do not enjoy any rights or any share -- even a tiny share -- of employment, educational, and economic opportunities. They have no choice but to pay bribes and endure various forms of humiliation and oppression.[1]

In tomorrow's Iran, where workers, farmers, and hardworking people in cities and villages are the driving force behind progress, development, and prosperity, all anti-worker and anti-farmer laws and regulations, as well as all debts to the Khomeini regime by farmers and workers, will be annulled. Instead, new rules will be adopted with their participation as the actual owners of their hard work.

In tomorrow's Iran, the expertise, intellect, and artistry of all patriotic experts, intellectuals, and artists, regardless of their global whereabouts, will be welcomed with open arms to contribute to the building, prosperity, advancement, and independence of the country, and to serve the welfare of its people.

Therefore, their thoughts, expertise, and efforts will be considered the most valuable human and national assets.

In tomorrow's Iran, national markets and investments, private and personal ownership, and investment leading to national economic development and production growth will be firmly established.

In tomorrow's Iran, priority will be given to meeting the basic needs of life, such as livelihood, housing, health, and education, for the underprivileged and low-income groups of society, including workers, farmers, and employees, particularly teachers, professors, and retirees.[2]

In tomorrow's Iran, national markets and investments, private and personal ownership, and investment leading to national economic development and production growth will be firmly established

Notes:

1- Maryam Rajavi's statement on the 70th anniversary of the Universal Declaration of Human Rights, December 2017; https://www.maryam-rajavi.com/en/declaration-by-maryam-rajavi-on-the-70th-anniversary-of-the-adoption-of-the-universal-declaration-of-human-rights/

2- "Freedom," Maryam Rajavi's speech in Dortmund, Germany, June 16, 1995

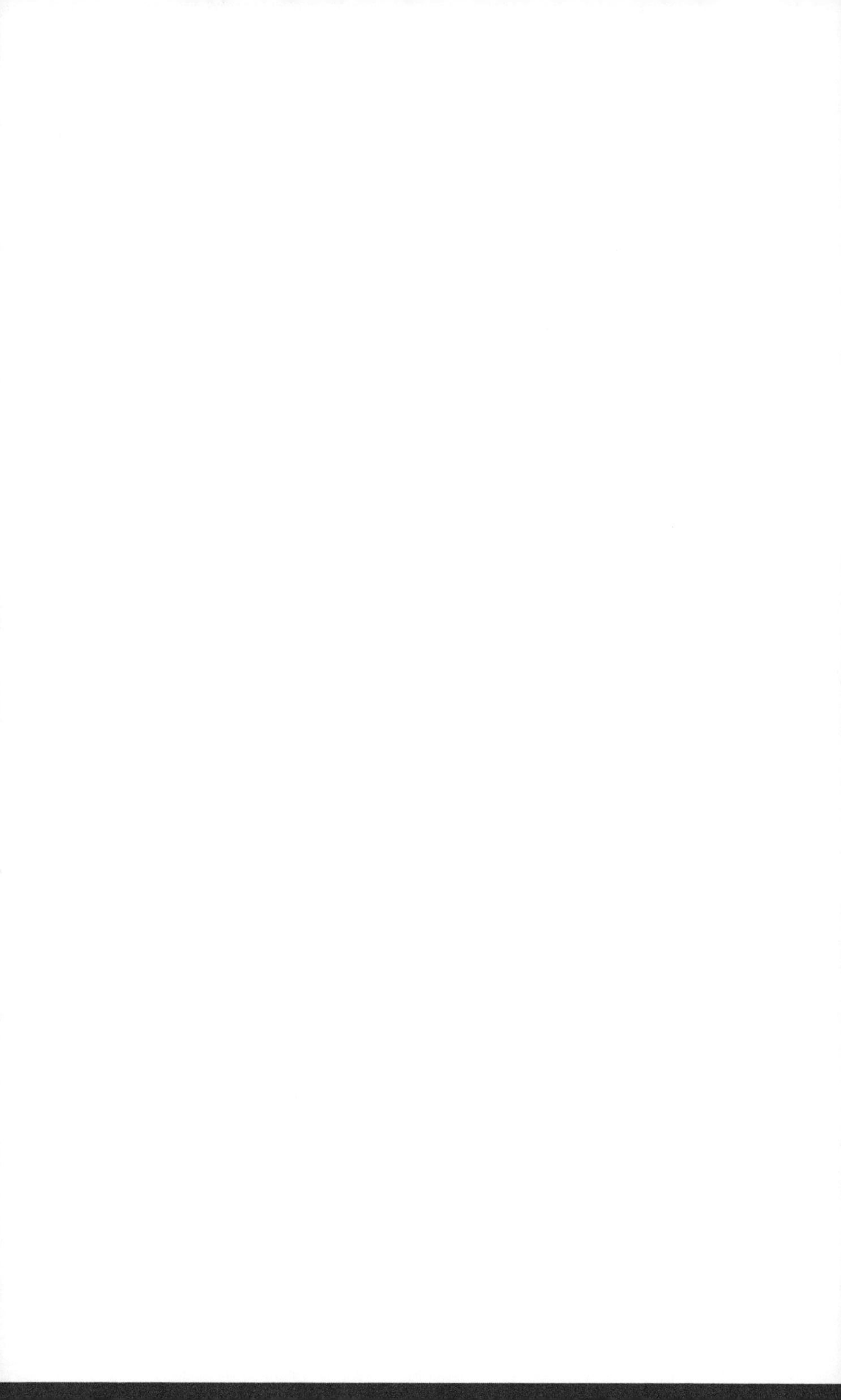

09

Protection and rehabilitation of the environment, decimated under the mullahs' rule.

Environmental disaster in Iran

It is possible to eradicate high prices, poverty, unemployment, shanty towns, water shortages, and environmental calamities. But before anything else, the trampled political rights, specifically the right to sovereignty of the Iranian people, must be restored and revived. This is the aim of our Resistance and the raison d'etre of the NCRI.[1]

Khomeini and his accomplices initiated their rule by crushing freedom, establishing their regime on the blood of Iranian fighters and victims of the 1967 massacre, and expanding their oppression and destruction in all aspects of society. They presided over the deterioration of education, culture, art, and

The tyranny and oppression have removed every obstacle to the death and destruction of Iran's environment by the ruling occupiers, the mullahs

morality, leading to economic collapse, environmental destruction, war, and terrorism against neighboring countries. The very concept of the Supreme Leader's rule implies increasing destruction and decay. The tyranny and oppression have removed every obstacle to the death and destruction of Iran's environment by the ruling occupiers, the mullahs.

In Iran, water scarcity and drought in some regions have led to dire circumstances and alarming prospects. One of Iran's largest lakes, Urmia, is amid an unprecedented decline, and wetlands are becoming a rarity. Forests have been mercilessly decimated while the spread of deserts and arid regions continues unabated. In several cities, the air quality has become intolerable, and the military and security agendas, as well as the exploitative projects of the Revolutionary Guards, have further devastated Iran's already depleted natural resources.[2]

Notes:

1- Maryam Rajavi's speech to the Iranian Resistance's Grand Rally in Paris, June 30, 2018; https://www.maryam-rajavi.com/en/regime-overthrow-is-certain-iran-will-be-free/

2- Maryam Rajavi's message to the demonstration in Paris, "Saving Human Rights and the Environment in Iran Depends on Regime Change," December 2017; https://www.maryam-rajavi.com/en/message-of-maryam-rajavi-to-the-iranians-demonstration-in-paris/

10

A non-nuclear Iran
that is also devoid
of weapons of mass
destruction.
Peace, co-existence and
international and regional
cooperation.

We want a non-nuclear Iran

In June 1991, when virtually nobody had any information about the regime's nuclear projects, the NCRI launched its extensive attempts to expose those projects.

In the early 2000s, the NCRI divulged documents which revealed the regime's 18-year clandestine nuclear weapons project. We took major strides on this path with the motto of a "non-nuclear Iran."[1]

Let me recall that the Iranian Resistance obtained documents regarding the secret negotiations of the regime's leaders in 1990, in which Rafsanjani declared that acquiring nuclear weapons was essential to the regime's survival.

On August 11, 2002, when our Resistance for the first time revealed the regime's nuclear projects in Natanz and Arak, we again announced what Rafsanjani, as president of the regime at the time, had said at a meeting of the Supreme National Security Council: "Acquiring nuclear weapons is the most important guarantee for our survival so that Western countries will not be able to prevent the Islamic revolution's spread of influence and advancement."

After Khomeini's death, Khamenei linked his and his regime's fate to the nuclear program, just as Khomeini had linked his fate to the war against Iraq.

In contrast, the Iranian Resistance adopted the policy of disrupting the regime's plans. Since 1991, the NCRI has made successive revelations, and in 2002, it revealed to the world the mullahs' most secret and important nuclear sites. The clerical regime's leaders have repeatedly acknowledged that these revelations have had a decisive impact on preventing them from acquiring the bomb. It is a source of pride for the Iranian Resistance that, thanks to the sacrifices of its members and supporters inside Iran, it has been more effective than all governments and international institutions in preventing the regime from acquiring an atomic bomb.[2]

In the 2015 agreement, the P5+1 countries offered numerous incentives and concessions to the regime. Accordingly, the regime was allowed to preserve its enrichment program. The six UN Security Council resolutions were suspended, and the regime received a cash windfall.

Having received these concessions, the regime embarked on covert operations to complete its nuclear program. It has kept the main team of its nuclear researchers intact and active. Salehi, the head of the regime's Atomic Energy Organization, acknowledged that in the heavy water reactor in Arak, where the fuel tank pipes had been filled with concrete, they had secretly purchased and maintained similar pipes. He and Khamenei were the only persons who were aware of this operation.

Multiple developments and evidence confirm that the regime began accelerating the completion of its nuclear program before the U.S. withdrawal from the nuclear deal. In the same year that the agreement was signed, the Internal Security Agency of the German state of North Rhine-Westphalia announced that it had recorded 141 attempts by the Iranian regime to purchase equipment for its nuclear program. German intelligence services have revealed in other documented reports that in each of the years since the signing of the JCPOA, the Iranian regime attempted to purchase materials and technology from German companies to build weapons of mass destruction.

In reality, the regime used the nuclear deal as a ceasefire in a war in which it was on the verge of defeat, in order to revitalize and expand its atomic program. In May 2017, Rouhani published a book in which he wrote that if the situation before the agreement had persisted, "a large-scale military attack by the enemy would not have been necessary, because the country would have collapsed from within."

With what I have briefly explained, it is clear how the regime continued to advance towards developing an atomic bomb at every step by deceiving the world and receiving concessions.

The result is that Khamenei is building a bomb and will not stop. Any agreement he signs to reduce these activities, and any promise he makes, are pure lies.[3]

Khamenei is building a bomb and will not stop. Any agreement he signs to reduce these activities, and any promise he makes, are pure lies

Notes:

1- Maryam Rajavi's speech at the 3-day summit of the National Council of Resistance of Iran marking the 40th anniversary of the NCRI's foundation, July 23-26, 2020; https://www.maryam-rajavi.com/en/maryam-rajavi-ncri-democratic-alternative-solution-future-iran/

2- Maryam Rajavi's speech to the second session of the Free Iran World Summit, July 11, 2021; https://www.maryam-rajavi.com/en/strategy-bomb-missiles-executioner-doomed-failure-second-day-free-iran-world-summit/

3 - Maryam Rajavi's speech to the second session of the Free Iran World Summit, July 11, 2021; https://www.maryam-rajavi.com/en/strategy-bomb-missiles-executioner-doomed-failure-second-day-free-iran-world-summit/